SOCIAL MEDIA
MASTERY

A Simple Formula For Busy Business
Owners And Entrepreneurs To Generate
Millions Of Impressions Online For Free

DREWBIE WILSON

SOCIAL MEDIA MASTERY

A Simple Formula For Busy Business Owners And Entrepreneurs To Generate Millions Of Impressions Online FOR FREE!
All Rights Reserved

Cover Design By: Rica Cabrex

Edited By: Drewbie Wilson, Andy Garrison, fatima_alishba

Dedication

To my wife, Kayla, the Madame of Memes, thank you for supporting me on this wild ride of social media. I know it wasn't easy to understand at first, but building this online empire together by learning to master these platforms has opened doors and taken us places we'd never imagined…

Thank you for believing in me!

El Duderino, you have yet to learn the extent of it. Still, you've been an enormous help in building our family's online empire. Keep snapping those excellent photos and sharing your ways of teaching people to Crush The Day!

To Ryan Stewman, the Hardcore Closer, thank you for showing me and countless others how to use social media to create generational wealth.

Thank you for spreading the message of becoming the greatest version of yourself and extracting greatness from everyone you come across.

It's an honor to teach people how to change their lives using the same wisdom you shared with me.

Thank you to the reader for taking the time to read this book and implement what you learn. Time is your most valuable resource, and for you to spend a little with me here means the world!

Resources

To learn more about Drewbie, his other books, podcasts, and for more content that can help you in becoming a social media master check out the following links.

1. www.drewbiewilson.com
2. www.connectwithdrewbie.com
3. www.Phonesites.com/drewbie
4. www.jointheapex.com
5. www.callthedamnleads.com

Contents

Foreword

This book started as an idea less than 2 weeks ago.

Drewbie came to me and said he was gonna write a book, make a funnel for it, and have it published in like 10 days.

Normally, a CEO would nod in agreement knowing the person they just agreed with has ZERO chances of delivering on that promise.

Not me though, I have known Andrew Wilson for over 3 years now and I know when he says he's gonna make something happen he does it.

Drewbie has proven time and time again to take unexpected challenges and rise to them.

He ran a whole-ass marathon with minimal training and preparation. He just fucking did it.

He rode over 200 miles on a bike in one setting. He just hopped on that fucker and rode until the wheels came off, literally.

The best part about all of this stuff like the book, the marathon, and the 200 miles is that it was all on social media.

This means it not only helped Drewbie physically, making posts about this stuff also helped him financially.

People online get to see him pushing himself and his upper limits. This inspires them to want to know more of how he does it. From there, he teaches them our processes and enrolls them into Apex.

It's a process he has perfected with 8 figures in proven sales with receipts to prove it.

This book is that process and how you can duplicate the efforts and wisdom you're about to read.

Enjoy the book, but more importantly do the fucking work.

Rise Above

Preface

The digital revolution has transformed marketing and taken it to a new level.

My name is Drewbie Wilson, and I have designed this book to impart great wisdom in your life regarding the value of social media for business owners and entrepreneurs.

I am the Vice President of both Break Free Academy and the Apex Mastermind Program, and I have a wealth of experience in harnessing social media's power to build your brand and make more money.

Using social media as my primary form of marketing and brand building, I've been able to generate thousands of leads online across a myriad of industries, including Insurance, Real Estate, Mortgage, Contracting, Roofing, Financial Services, Consulting, etc. I could go on, but you get the point.

From those leads, I have personally closed more than **$13,000,000** in sales online, and the clients we've worked with, a whole heck of a lot more than that!

As a savvy business owner, you understand social media's essential role in modern-day life. With 4.7 billion active users, most of your potential clients are already engaging with these platforms daily and, on average, spend two hours per day browsing through the plethora of content available. This makes organic social media an ideal way to generate revenue while having an impactful presence.

However, it can be challenging to become an expert in this field with limited time and resources. Fortunately, this book offers solutions to overcoming those challenges by providing strategies that will help you master organic social media without having to dedicate too much of your time each day. It covers the basics and more advanced concepts that can be applied to generate quality leads and convert them into paying customers by creating an effective online presence.

Learn how to easily create shareable content across social platforms and make sure your message reaches the right audience!

Let me give you a little background on my journey...

In 2018, I was an up-and-coming insurance producer for a family agency in Toledo, Ohio. I had been in the business for about five years. I slowly built up a small business book through cold calling, working my sphere of influence, and purchasing leads from our online vendors. These leads would cost us anywhere from $10 to $25 a piece, depending on how much information they provided and how recently it had come through.

If you've ever purchased leads online, you know what a time and money sink it can be. Between the wrong phone numbers and the misspelled emails, you're typically fighting against 3-5 other competitors in your area to be the first to close the sale. It can be a challenging way to make a living, but one that works if you know how to work.

Now, I'm not afraid of a little hard work. Still, I was also taught that there is usually an easier way of doing things if you take a moment to step back and educate yourself. Or, as the quote goes, "Give me four hours to chop down a tree, and I'll spend the first three sharpening my ax." Stepping back to get a deeper understanding of social media and how it worked was my version of sharpening the ax.

In the same way, I figured out how to work internet leads with a strong pre-qualification and follow-up process; I learned how to use social media to make sure my products and services were being shown to the correct audience.

I had been online in the Sales Talk With Sales Pros Facebook community, a private Facebook group of sales professionals, for about six months, following along with other insurance agents and trying to see if I could pick up any ideas on what they were doing to generate leads on the platform.

Eventually, I reached out to one individual who was a representative for a company that offered to teach insurance agents how to build a marketing campaign to get highly qualified leads using social media. At the end of our call, he hit me with the price…

"$1500 paid in full. There are no payment options because we need to know you're committed."

"Well, shit!" I thought to myself…

I didn't have that kind of money readily available at the time. Funds were limited with a wife, a young son, and a newly signed mortgage agreement. So I asked the guys if they could give me a day or two to get the funds together. They agreed, and I returned to the agency's owner to discuss the opportunity.

"Absolutely Not… Just stick to the tried and true. Go buy some more leads."

Let's say the owner did not share my enthusiasm for the tactics I saw online and in these private insurance producer communities on social media.

When I called back a few days later, I had decided I would front the cost out of my pocket to learn this skill and bank on the added commissions from all the sales I'd be making to offset the investment.

"Sorry, we already sold your slot to someone else."

I was crushed…

I'm not sure; maybe you're like me or not, but when someone tells me it's too late or that my opportunity has passed, I don't take it too lightly. So when these fellas let me know I could not sign up for their program, my FIGURE IT TF OUT genes kicked into overdrive. I knew this wasn't the end of my journey into mastering social media marketing.

I had been following Ryan Stewman and the Sales Talk group for a while, meaning he and I had built a good rapport. So when he launched his new, easier-to-use website-building software, I was one of the first 100 users to sign up for the Phonesites platform. As a struggling insurance agent, I used it to generate leads for my agency.

In the first few months, We were able to generate hundreds of leads for our agency, and I was able to nearly double my monthly production. This was the beginning of my journey in learning how to utilize social media effectively—taking time to dial in on the ins and outs of marketing and what drives engagement on social media.

Joining the Apex mastermind was a HUGE help in learning these skills.

I eventually built a marketing company with one of the guys I met in the community that did pretty well, doing multiple five-figures in business, before selling my part to that same partner about a year later. All the while working behind the scenes as a support member for the company. Over time I'd work my way up the ladder to be the now Vice President at Break Free Academy.

I'm proud to say that during my time as an agency owner and Phonesites user, I was the number one affiliate for a while. However, when my focus shifted to the Apex Mastermind Program, I may have lost that title. But despite that, my passion for using social media to drive business success remains more vital than ever, and my love for the Phonesites platform is still there! This entire book was built from the foundation of a presentation I gave to that community on implementing the exact steps I am showing you here!

Through this book, I want to help you become a social media master, potentially using it to generate millions of dollars in revenue for your business. I want you to use these tactics to build your professional presence online and see how these strategies can help you make a **massive impact** on your community. We'll be talking about the intentional usage of social media and how you can take your personal AND professional life to the next level. So, let's get started!

I'm excited to share my insights on social media mastery for busy business owners and entrepreneurs. As an author, husband, and father, I understand the importance of balancing work with personal life and the value of time. I'm also an intrapreneur within the Apex community, building multiple brands and businesses on social media using the same simple formulas I will share in this book. So I feel confident that I have a pretty good understanding of how to teach them to you.

Think of these formulas and strategies like grandma's famous cookie recipe.

> *You know, if you trust the process, you'll end up with something that resembles a childhood favorite!*

Over time, you will add flavor and spice to the recipe to make it your own. The more you focus on being original and adding your authentic style, the more you will increase your engagement with the target audience! If you give a prospect a cookie... Well, you know what happens next!

My passion for social media stems from my firsthand experience in using it to drive results for my businesses. I spend about an hour or two on social media daily. Still, by being intentional with my usage, I've generated thousands of leads and helped others do the same.

I've seen the impact of intentional social media usage firsthand, such as with a jeweler who received 265 organic leads in just 24 hours. He could only have done that by building the know, like, and trust factor with his audience. As we already know, those three things are paramount to creating a significant business transaction!

Social media has enormous potential, with billions of users online daily. My goal is to show you how you can harness that potential to drive revenue for your business. By using social media with intention and purpose, you can get a substantial return on your investment without sacrificing all of your valuable time.

As you will learn, time is your most valuable asset, and the better you invest it, the bigger your R.O.I will be!

It is time to take your social media game to the next level!

Why Social Media?

"Social networks aren't about web sites. They are about experience!"
Mike DiLorenzo

As I mentioned, there are more people online every day than people in your town. You only need a small percentage of those people to know who you are, like you enough to follow your profile, and trust you enough to do business with or send you business to make life-changing money and impact.

To connect with your ideal client, you need to understand their behavior and presence on social media platforms. Utilizing these platforms allows you to engage in meaningful conversations and build relationships with your target audience. This method is cost-effective as it only requires time and effort to create and publish engaging content.

There's no need to spend money you don't have on advertising, as all you need to do is share your story and establish rapport with your audience. By doing so, you can establish a connection based on trust, which is crucial in converting potential clients into paying customers.

By focusing on your ideal client and consistently delivering value through social media, you can become the go-to expert in your industry. Mat Smith, who leveraged social media to become the referral king for contractor marketing, demonstrates this well. He shows up online as his authentic self. He pours value into the community by educating them on the pro's and con's of marketing. Then entertains them with his hilarious stories and fantastic copywriting ability.

By capturing customer data using Phonesites and utilizing it to provide the best possible services for their needs, Mat has established a reputation as a trusted and knowledgeable resource in the community. By following this process, you, too, can become the referral king or queen in your marketplace.

To cultivate a dedicated following of raving fans, it's crucial to create an accessible platform for them to share their referrals with you. To do this, you must first dial in on WHO your ideal client is. When we go into a business to consult on the sales process, we first ask what we are helping and WHAT their B.H.A.P (Big Hairy Ass Problem) is?

Knowing whom you want to do business with and attract online is the first step in becoming a social media master!

When you think about it hard, you already know that not all business is good business...

For example, you could be getting your start in real estate and think, I am looking to do business with anyone who wants to buy or sell their home. You're absolutely right! You can service those individuals, but what if I came to you holding a list of 100 trailer owners who wanted to sell their trailers for $5,000 - $10,000?

Would you still be interested in taking on the business? Probably not...

Unless your ideal client is a trailer park owner looking to fill their empty lots with units to rent out.

If you're an up-and-coming agent, that's probably not the case. However, there may be someone who figures out that there is a market for this and goes on to create their sub-niche in the game. Kudos to that person for taking action!

Back to my point... You will realize you don't want to do business with everyone. You want to get very clear about the type of business you want to focus on and the type of individual who will be easy to work with while having the problem you are an expert at solving.

When you know you're looking to work with investors who want multi-unit properties in the $500,000 - $1,000,000 range with a school in a 5-mile radius, you can get more dialed in on the marketing message and the content you create. This will ensure the folks who actively follow and engage with your content fit this category as closely as possible.

For everyone else, they become your online army of referral machines!

You see, only some people who follow you or engage with your content online will be your ideal client. That doesn't mean you should forget about them, though! As I mentioned before, this process of social media mastery is about more than just making money online, and it's about making an impact.

The more impact you make in someone's life, the more respect and appreciation they have for you. That impact could be as simple as the motivational posts you put out daily or the entertaining stories you share about your family adventures.

The stories keep you top of mind, and when someone who appreciates the effort you put into your content hears another person mention a need for your product or service, you'll be the person who gets tagged in their post online or noted as someone who can be trusted to help.

Receiving referrals from friends, family, and your trusted followers can be the difference between your business making it through the hard times, and failing in the first couple years. The more you take care of your clients and provide them the highest quality of services, the more likely they are to tell others about you and your business.

The goal of using social media in this manner is to build your network of potential referral partners. This is going to help you generate more referrals both online, and offline because the followers you have will be seeing your content more often, therefore keeping you top of mind when someone mentions a need for your professional services.

REFERRALS ARE THE BEST LEADS YOU CAN GET!

Setting up a simple Phonesites page allows for easy and efficient tracking of these referrals. This not only helps you establish a solid network of potential clients, but it also enables you to show appreciation for those who send you business by keeping track of their contributions.

By acknowledging and rewarding those who support your business, you can strengthen your relationships and foster a community of loyal supporters who want to see you succeed.

Your supporters can send you referrals if you make a simple Phonesites page where they can send you the information. You can then reach out to that referral and find out what problems they have and if you're a good fit to help solve them. By tracking the referrals, you can even gift the supporters. I like to do nice things for others who send me business, and keeping track of those who do the same for you, would help you do the same for them.

You might say, "Hey, I got another lead from Jessica over at the insurance agency. Let's make sure we send her a gift card."

There are many ways to build that authority in your market, as you do you'll want a simple way to collect data and stay organized; Phonesites is a great way to help simplify that process.

> **Now, how many of you want an employee who works 24/7/365, and is constantly sparking out revenue-generating opportunities?**

All of you.

I know that. I was that guy.

I'm here because I understand that if you build these systems right, you have 24-hour-a-day advertisements going out to the world.

Now, here's the thing, we know that you can't just spam people all day long.

We know that we can't just slap them over the head with our offers and the things we do for people, or eventually, they will stop coming around.

In the following chapters, I will explain the simple way to keep your audience engaged in your content without making them feel turned off by an overly sales'y approach.

IS YOUR PROFILE GENERATING SALES FOR YOUR BUSINESS?

It's Free Real Estate

It's Not What Ya Know,
It's Who Ya Know!

"Your Network Is Your Net Worth!"
-Porter Gale-

N etworking is crucial to building a successful business, as it provides opportunities to connect with potential clients, partners, and allies. Traditional networking often involves spending time and resources, such as coffee meetings or BNI group memberships, to establish relationships and build a network.

By utilizing social media platforms and tools like Phonesites, you can streamline this process and reach a wider audience while saving time and resources. However, it's important to remember that networking is not just about acquiring new contacts, but also about fostering genuine relationships based on mutual support and trust.

What you have to remember is that we're building a networking opportunity. We're taking all that time we spend meeting people for coffee, trying to start a relationship like, "Hey, can we meet and have dinner? Can we have drinks? Can we have coffee? I'd love to send you some business. I'd love to learn how we can support each other." You also join BNI groups and other networking communities. We spend so much time meeting different people, meeting strangers, trying to build a network. If you think about it, going to the coffee shop costs time and money too. Driving across town multiple times a week uses a lot of gas… and the time you lost? Forget about it!

But what if you built your coffee shop?

What if you had one central place where people could stop and get to know you?

Maybe create some rapport, hear a little bit of your story, see some of the things you're up to, and get an opportunity to see if they like you. Ultimately, suppose they feel that they trust you enough to want to do business together. In that case, you will have succeeded in your goal because that's what we're doing here in every one of these situations.

Whether posting content online or going and meeting someone in person, we're trying to establish, do I know this person?

Do I want to know them?

Am I going to like them?

And ultimately, can I trust them enough to be vulnerable with and for them to solve my problems?

Building trust with your audience is vital to creating a successful and sustainable business. That trust building process is so much more than posting about how great you are and how much success you have. It comes back to being honest and vulnerable, being relatable to the people who follow you. Your struggle is your story and the story is what people tell others.

The majority of the world wants to see others win. Putting out the good, the bad, the ugly, and everything in between adds a layer of trust that most businesses don't have with their clients. When someone trusts you, they are more likely to refer you to their friends and family, which is a valuable form of marketing.

If I like them, do I trust them? If I trust them, can I trust them with my friends, family members, and the people who are important to me?

Because that's what referrals are, a guarantee for someone else's ability to do the job and meet expectations. However, if you refer someone to another vendor and that vendor does not meet expectations, your reputation can be tarnished. This highlights the importance of having a platform where you can consistently engage with your audience and build the know, like, and trust factor.

You can quickly establish trust and cultivate a loyal following by having a place for people to learn about your business and interact with you on their terms. This system follows a know, like, and trust process that generates leads by helping you become the authority and trusted expert in your space.

First Impressions Matter

"You never get a second chance to make a first impression."
– Will Rogers

Your profile is your digital handshake!

Why is it essential for your digital handshake to make sense and to be strong?

How many of you have met a stranger with a limp handshake or an awkward demeanor? Are we shaking? Are we high-fiving or elbowing?

Remember, during COVID, you had to do the elbow thing?

Initial introductions can be uncomfortable. And even then, when you have that initial introduction, there is a parallel mental process where you walk in, and you're like,

"All right, who am I meeting? I want to see this person. Do they look sketchy? Is it someone that will make me immediately turn around and walk back out?"

That's how it almost always happens.

People want to know whom they're doing business with, so it's vital that you have your profile photo set up this way.

Human nature is to operate in Fight or Flight mode.

Suppose your online presence immediately throws a red flag in the viewer's mind. In that case, it will be exponentially harder to earn their trust. Think about all the referrals that people send you! If you get tagged in a post, and that person goes to see your profile, it's a hot mess...

Let's make sure that's never the case for you!

In this section, we will streamline your profile and assist you in ensuring that your first impression is the best! The section includes the following;

- A deconstruction of your profile into all important bits and pieces
- A guide to a attention-retaining Profile Picture
- Making a suitable Banner to represent you

- Detailed guides to how you should introduce different aspects of your life
- Specifying job roles and generalizing addresses
- Building a Social Proof
- Entering 'The Funnel': Taking people to the next level of doing business

Profile Deconstruction

Glamour Shots

"The best thing about a picture is that it never changes, even when the people in it do."
Andy Warhol

Your profile picture is the first thing that draws a visitor's attention. It can make or break your deal by retaining the viewer's attention, which is why I emphasize the need for an appropriate Profile Picture. But what do I mean by that?

In this section, I will demonstrate the right type and way of putting up a profile picture.

It all begins with quality, so make sure your profile picture is a clear picture of you. People want to know whom they're doing business with. Please don't do the whole real estate thing where you have your glamor shot from the '80s when it's 2023, and you don't look anything like that.

A lack of congruence in your branding online is a quick way to diminish any credibility you've built with prospective clients.

Again, we may only initially have 30-45 seconds of this person's attention, and we want to do everything in our power to keep them engaged.

Have a clear, concise photo of yourself.

Don't keep a logo. Nor a picture of your dog.

Don't have your brokerage's name on there or your company's branding. People don't buy from logos or corporations.

People buy from people that they know, like, and trust. If you're going to be that individual, put it out there and be your authentic self.

Almost every person on the planet has a phone capable of taking HIGH-QUALITY photos and headshots. Get rid of that fuzzy, hard-to-see picture, and create a picture of yourself that you can be proud of!

As we mentioned, not all good business is good business. It will be easier for you to weed out those who aren't a good fit by creating a solid digital handshake that represents your mission accordingly.

> *Them looking into your photo as if it was your face during a natural handshake is critical!*

Let me give you a hack...

You can see I've got a picture of myself and my beautiful wife for a profile picture because people are creeps, and social media is designed for people to creep. When people see this picture, they're going to click on it, and they're going to want to see,

> *"Hey, Who's this lady? Does this guy have a good-looking wife? What's going on here?"*
>
> *The entire goal of that initial 30-second introduction is to keep people's attention!*

If they're clicking through to see my wife and what she looks like, they'll know that she's beautiful and unique and be like,

> *"Damn, this guy's a closer. I want to know him because he's got something going on if he could pull her."*

Because I'm goofy, and that also makes me relatable. I've got something going on that people can see and want to learn about—especially my primary audience, males between the ages of 25 and 55. So I already know in their mind what they are thinking and what problems they are likely dealing with. This means I am doing my best to speak directly to the things that interest me, verbally or via the imagery I put out in my content.

But if it were just a picture of our dog, people wouldn't trust that.

They might think, I'm not going to do business with a dog. I don't care how cute it is; that dog can't solve my problem. Unless their problem is needing another dog, that's a different conversation for another day.

Now, when it comes to many of the social platforms, you not only have a primary profile photo, there is a second banner section you are given with open real estate to provide more insight into who you are and what you're about.

Find out how to leverage that portion of your profile in the next chapter.

Agent Profile   **Reality**

The Banner Flag

Hoist The Jolly Roger!
- Blackbeard

What is the thing that compliments your profile photo?

The banner or cover in your profile!

Make this something that's relatable. Share some of your hobbies, your interests. People aren't there to see a billboard and be sold on

'We're the number one brokerage in Kansas.'

Their reaction will most likely be:

Okay, cool. That doesn't matter. Are they voted by who?
Doesn't matter. These are all made-up titles and awards
90% of the time.

At least, that's what I see… Maybe because I have seen thousands of the same kind of profiles over the years, all of them look like cookie-cutter templates made by someone who loves talking about themselves and their achievements.

Please don't make it a billboard.

Please don't make it spammy.

Make it authentic... That's what people want!

If you look at my banner, it says a lot about me. At least enough for people to be curious. Their stream of thoughts may go like this:

> *Drewbie loves his wife because she's in two pictures on his profile, and he must love his son too. So he's a family man... Crush the Day, what's that all about? Oh, that's his brand. That's cool.*

This is just their initial thought. They haven't even moved past the first third of the screen yet. They're already having this internal conversation with themselves, much like when you walk into the coffee shop, When you go to shake that person's hand. You're going to make a choice on how you proceed.

In marketing, we call it "above the fold," which refers to the newspaper headlines and doing your best to look attractive and grab attention in that top section. When you walk in to shake someone's hand, you go through this internal process...

> *You're looking them up and down. Do they smell? Ugh, they got a smell to them. I knew it was going to be like this… Are their nails trimmed? Man, this guy didn't wash his hands. I gotta get out of here!*

You're making all of these initial judgments based on looks alone, and this same happens when someone clicks through to your profile and looks at your content on social media. People are always making those snap judgments, so do your best not to give them a reason to immediately cut and run away when they land on your page.

Real Estate agents be talking about, "I'm the #1 producer in the brokerage!" and be the only MFs in the brokerage...

Tell Me About Yourself...

"No Name, No Fame!"
– My Son's Teacher

First and foremost, it's important to remind you that you should use your real name and information for social media. One of the fastest ways to create confusion or a lack of credibility with your audience is to use a fake name or profile online to build your business. When potential clients find out you're using a phony name, they will have questions...

Why is this person using a fake name?

What do they have to hide?

Did they get in trouble for something they did, and they don't want me to know?

Did they steal from their previous clients?

You don't want to put yourself in a position of misleading your clients right off the bat.

The other side is that you want to ensure your branding is in line.

Drewbie probably sounds funny when you say it the first couple of times. You also have to say it a couple of times to make sure you say it correctly, which means you're forcing yourself to remember it. That's an internal hook. Suppose I were to tell you my name was Andrew, my actual name. In that case, you'd probably be thinking, *OK, Andy, Drew, Andrew,* whatever little nicknames you put on people when they have a dull or standard name.

The name Drewbie comes from when I was an online gamer, and my friends in the gaming community started calling me it. It carried over to when I was in the commodities relocation business. OK, I was selling drugs, but the previous sounds more legitimate. Most people who came to know me in that world knew me by the name Drewbie, so it just stuck with me as I moved into social media. Because the people who KNOW me know me by the name Drewbie, I have stuck with it for the last decade or more.

My personal branding helps people remember me and to stay top of mind.

If you have a nickname or a moniker that people know you by, use that previously built personal branding and lean into it. As you learn, people buy from people they KNOW, LIKE, and TRUST.

Make them feel as though they are getting to know the real you on social media.

The next thing people inquire after, "What's your name?" Is "What do you do?"

This is the time for your 30-second elevator pitch, describing who you are and what you're known for.

As per my profile, I'm Drewbie Wilson.

I inspire success-driven winners to become the most elite version of themselves by teaching them to crush the day.

"That's kind of cool. I'm into that." the person may think.

But if my response to that question was,

"Ah, well, I coach people and mentor and speak. I own a software company and have some other stuff going on. And then I hang out with my wife and kids sometimes."

That sort of response sounds overwhelming or less than confident. It needs to be a more straightforward and more confident response. Establishing rapport and credibility as quickly as possible during that initial conversation would be best.

During that first conversation, building rapport and establishing the know, like, and trust factor is essential. You can talk about your mission, what sets you apart, and what you bring to the table. You can also share stories that demonstrate your expertise and highlight your successes.

The key is to be relatable and connect with the person you're speaking with. Show them that you understand their needs and offer value that will benefit them. Doing so will lay the foundation for a productive and potentially profitable relationship.

Your ideal response to a profile should be closer to,

> *Hey, this is someone I can respect. This is someone that I'm confident in just based on their initial appearance. Even if I don't know them that well yet, just them showing up the way they have makes me feel more comfortable if I am in a situation where I'm thinking about potentially doing business with them.*

Suppose you've built enough rapport with your prospects at that first glance. In that case, they look over your profile and banner image to make sure you aren't sketchy, and seeing your name, they should continue moving on to learn more about you, such as what you do and why.

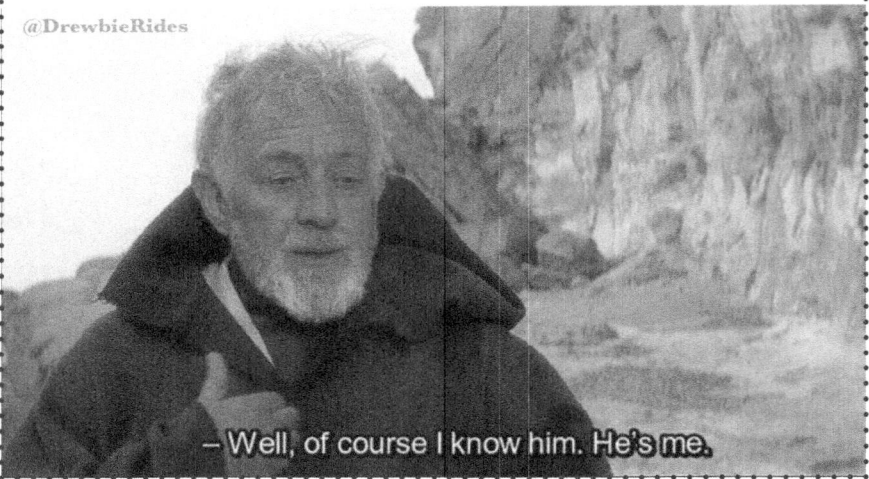

When Someone Asks If I Heard About The Guy Who Made Multiple Millions In Sales With Memes...

@DrewbieRides

— Well, of course I know him. He's me.

Get You A J.O.B!

"Do your job; be the best at whatever your job description is."
Randy Moss

Y ou have to be specific about what you do and how you help people... *I'm the vice president at Apex Entourage.* **I have one main job.**

Do I have five other ancillary businesses that I also run and consult for?

Yes, 100%. But if I mentioned all of those things in our first conversation, what would happen?

> *This guy does not know what he is doing. Is he a real estate*
> *agent, or is he an insurance agent? Is he a business broker?*
> *He's got nine different jobs. What is this guy great at?*

Because when you have multiple previous jobs or skills listed, people might think you're good at everything but not great at anything. Or worse, they may think you suck at everything, which why you can't hold a job. I'm not saying that's you, but we don't want to leave any room for confusion.

You don't want to be the jack of all trades, master of none. You have one specific job that you focus on and are an expert in. Don't put all of your past jobs on your profile. Pick the things that matter to your ideal client, and focus on those only.

Narrowing down and focusing on your primary skills is critical for success. It can be tempting to spread yourself thin and try to do too many things but becoming an expert in one area sets you apart as a leader and innovator. Being able to answer the question "what are you an expert in?" shows people that you have intricate knowledge of that field and inspires confidence.

Knowing how to focus your energy will help you make lasting impacts while opening up opportunities to become even more specialized. Ultimately, it is better to be great at a few things than just okay at many.

Trust me when I say you're going to hear over and over that millionaires have multiple income streams. That **might** be true for some people, but don't fall into the trap of thinking you need to show the world how many different jobs you have. You want them to know you as the expert in one thing from a place they are familiar with.

Where Ya From, Kid?

"Home Is Not Where You Live, But Where They Understand You"
– Christian Morgenstern

W here are you from?

Me?, I'm from Dallas, Texas.

Technically, we live over in the suburbs of Plano. Still, people I work with don't typically know Plano. I work with people from around the world, so it's easier to say Dallas because it's more central, and most people know Dallas. There's an instant connection there, relatability.

If I said I was from some random small town in Ohio, you might not think of me as someone who knows how to handle big-city clients.

On the flip side of that, if you're trying to become the most known person in YOUR SMALL TOWN, then yes, 100% it's important for people to know that you live there and are an upstanding member of the community.

> *Having geographic familiarity is essential for sales, as it can be the difference between getting a deal or not.*

The first way it is crucial is by creating an instant connection with potential customers.

Knowing the city that someone lives in and talking about it in familiar terms allows them to feel both comfortable and understood. They may also be more likely to trust someone who brings up areas they are already familiar with rather than someone who does not have any geographical knowledge.

Another way geographic familiarity helps in sales is by building client relationships. Building relationships takes time, but understanding where a customer is from can help you establish those connections more quickly.

Understanding the culture and climate of a particular area can give you an edge when trying to show that you genuinely care about your customers' needs and concerns; this helps build loyalty and trust between the two parties.

Finally, having geographic familiarity can help in setting expectations when it comes to sales.

Knowing where a person lives gives you better insight into their needs so that you can tailor your approach accordingly. You can also use local references to gain credibility and establish yourself as an expert in your field, making customers more likely to trust your product or service, even if it's unfamiliar.

These conversation points create successful sales strategies that will lead to more conversions.

Remember, your profiles are set up to attract and speak to your ideal client.

These strategies are moldable to your specific client's avatar and needs, making them effective. Your profile should flow smoothly from one piece to the next, making the viewer feel good.

As we know, to build the know, like, and trust factor with clients, we want them to see us as easy to work with and that others have said it's easy to work with us too.

Almost like the reviews online you look for when picking a new restaurant.

If Enough People Say It's Good, It's Probably Not Bad...

"Just trust me dude"
- Some guy telling his buddy to eat the gas station sushi

If you land on my page and you don't know me that well, you may take a look and say, *"Oh, he's followed by several thousand people. That's interesting. Why?"*

Because the majority of people on social media only have a few hundred or so friends. So it should make you curious why so many people follow me online if we're not "friends."

Curiosity is precisely what we are looking for! We want to keep drawing these individuals further down the page and into our content stream.

Think about when you're choosing which restaurant to eat at or where to shop for a specific product/service. What do you do first?

TO THE GOOGLE MACHINE!!!

You start looking at the rating and the reviews, right?

You're more likely to go there if the company or location has a 4-5 star rating.

If you look and see that it has a 4-5 star rating, but there have only been four reviews, you may question it. If that location had hundreds of reviews all saying the same thing, the level of trust you would have for a good experience would be exponentially higher.

That's called social proof.

Seeing others talk about or being actively interested in a product or service gives us more confidence in getting a similar result. You can make people feel more comfortable with you based on social proof. In that case, you're making it much easier for someone to move from "interested" to "Paid In Full."

Social proof is essential for businesses to build trust and confidence with their customers. Customers are increasingly relying on the opinions of others to make decisions, especially when it comes to making a purchase.

When potential customers see that other people have had a positive experience, they are more likely to have a similar experience.

Social proof can come in many forms, such as customer reviews, testimonials, ratings, and endorsements from industry influencers. Reviews from previous customers provide detailed information about the product or service and give potential customers an accurate representation of what they can expect if they invest in it.

It's important for businesses to foster a positive relationship with their customers and ensure that any negative feedback is addressed quickly and professionally. It also helps if companies incentivize their current customers to leave reviews or give testimonials. This will help attract new customers who may not have been aware of the business.

Overall having social proof is beneficial for businesses as it allows them to build trust between themselves and their target audience by providing evidence that their products/services are worth investing in.

Additionally, having numerous positive reviews will help improve the visibility of a business online as more people become aware of its offerings. Lastly, having social proof can also lead to increased conversations around the brand which can be used as free marketing due to word-of-mouth recommendations passed on from one person to another.

Social Proof is a building block in making people comfortable enough to want to see your website. When you have hooked people to your profile, the next step is making them take the next step: Visit Your Website!

Therefore, it is time to move on to 'The Funnel.'

The Funnel

"Gotta Catch'em All!
- Ash Ketchum

T he climax of your profile visit is when and if the visitor clicks your website link. It is, therefore, crucial to make your website a selling strength.

As a business owner, you may be at the point where you ask yourself, 'Is my website good enough? Does it answer the questions my potential customers might have in mind?'
Let me share the story of my website: connectwithdrewbie.com.

As you can see, it's clean, professional, and easy to navigate, almost like a digital business card. It quickly communicates who Drewbie is and what I stand for and provides a clear call to action for anyone looking to connect with me further.

The website is an extension of my online presence. It serves as a hub to connect with me for all of my businesses and brands, effectively showcasing my expertise and thought leadership.

Having a website like this can build trust and credibility with your audience, further establishing you as a valuable resource in you industry while giving them a place to create a connection in their comfort.

Using this digital business card, I can collect prospect data and get them into our CRM as quickly as possible. This allows me to start the sales and follow-up process responsible for millions of dollars in revenue in our company each year.

Connectwithdrewbie.com is a website built on the Phonesites platform because I preach and use what I say and do.

One of our core values at Apex is Integrity. We do what we say we're going to do when we say we're going to do it, and I use Phonesites because if I'm going to tell our clients to use it, I will use it as well!

I also use all the unique gadgets and features that make it convenient to get this information out there. I'm using QR scanners, pulse cards, etc. I'm putting it out there because I recognize the value of this platform and its utility.

There are many ways to get out there and use this platform. But the digital business card, the intro setup they give you, and these templates are goldmines for marketing. I get leads almost daily from people who find me online, look at my profile, click on this website, text me, add me to their stuff, and buy my book.

That's what this is all about.

We're building a machine to generate opportunities and leads, then using Phonesites to capture their information.

In short, you're going to have a website, a straightforward location for people to get that additional information they need, and then, ideally, continue in the funnel to the sales process.

What's a funnel supposed to do?

It's supposed to take data from up here *imagine me holding my hands up in a giant Y formation* and funnel it down to where they become a potential prospect or a buying client. That's the simple truth.

We not only want them to buy from us or to use our service. We want them to follow us and see more of our content. So part of the process is using this funnel to help move people through the stages of your know, like, and trust process to the point of buying from you.

If they CAN'T buy from us, then at least they can be someone who learns and gets value from us by proxy of the content we share. You never know when those individuals could become your most significant referral resource!

If you can, the code below will take you directly to my digital business card, as you see above. It helps you understand how easy this process is to collect information from your clients during that initial online introduction. Because that's all we've done so far, is start the conversation.

QR CODE FOR

www.connectwithdrewbie.com

...All That For An Introduction!

"It's much easier to get a reception from someone if there is an introduction versus randomly trying to get in front of people."
– Brad Feld

First impressions are a big deal, just like when you meet someone for the first time at a coffee shop. And your social media profile is your digital handshake - it's the first impression you give to anyone who comes across your content online.

Ensuring your intro is rock solid and stands out is crucial. You want it to leave a substantial impact on people, whether they're scrolling through their feed during their workday or having late-night thoughts about life.

With a killer intro, you can be there for them when they need it. They may see a post you made earlier that hits them at the right time and place, and before you know it, you've got leads pouring in who want to learn more about how you can help solve their problems. That's what being in business is all about!

Make sure your profile is set up accordingly because this will be that initial judgment by someone who lands on your page and says,

"Yep, I'm all about it"

or

"Nope, I'm immediately right back out the door onto the next one."

When you've carefully crafted your profiles to be a strong representation of your mission and a solid digital handshake, you might get lucky enough to draw your audience to become a follower of your daily news channel!

Content Creation Process

What, Where, When to Post, and Why!

The News Feed Strategy

"An Exhibitionist Is Nothing Without A Voyeur."
– S.A.Saches

When you look at your social media profiles, you know there's a timeline of content being shared by yourself and the other users.

There is content constantly being put out there. 24/7/365 and then the extra day on leap years!

What does that mean? It means you are now the chief content creator of your news station or television channel.

However, you chose to relate to it. You are the person who's responsible for putting out all the news and stories regarding your life and times.

That's what social media was created for. It was designed so that other people could be creeps and live vicariously through the content you're putting out there. So they can watch your stuff and see all the things going on in your life.

They want to see your stories.

They want to know what you've got going on.

People love seeing pictures of the kids and hearing about what's happening.

One of the main concerns of a new content creator is,

"What should I post about?"

Think about what people like to see. People tend to scour through other people's social media timelines with a curious and discerning eye, searching for signs of personality, interests, and lifestyles.

We look for glimpses of creativity in the form of art and photography and seek out moments of humor and joy amidst the daily monotony.

Your followers are looking for evidence of intelligence, passion, and ambition in the form of captions and shared articles. And they search for authenticity, a genuine reflection of the person behind the screen, and the meaningful connections and relationships they have built with others.

People are drawn to unique stories and perspectives that can only be found on a social media timeline, making it a window into someone else's world. It will create that Know, Like, and Trust factor by giving a peek inside your life, values, and lessons.

With all that, a chance to use your incredible and valuable products or services!

This section includes;

- Strategies to solve that mammoth question of 'what to post?'
- Addresses your self-doubts about your content
- Introduces you to the F.O.R.M Method to keep your timeline busy
- More tried, tested and successful insider tools to rock your timeline!

Let Me Tell You A Little Story All About How...

"Whoever controls the media, controls the mind."
– Jim Morrison

D o you pay attention to the media content you consume?

Have you ever noticed how some news channels are specifically designed to put out a ton of very... What's the word I'm looking for? Divisive content.

They air political stuff.
They put out hatred and negativity.
They put out media and stories designed to elicit specific feelings and responses.

You could do that. But again, what you put out is what you attract. If you're putting out positive stories that inspire hope and success, that's what you'll see more of. If you put out the stuff that "triggers" people or causes them to react in an argumentative way or look for trouble, that's what you'll keep getting.

The algorithm is built this way on purpose.

The media has been using these methods since the dawn of media, and we're just learning how they've adapted them to the new world.

Suppose you start thinking about my timeline and the content I'm putting out. It needs to be a reflection of me and my mission. Then, that makes you fall in line with what your audience is tuned into.

Old W.I.I.F.M., *what's in it for me?* Radio, as the late, great Zig Ziglar called it.

People are always thinking about "What's in it for me?"

> *If I'm going to take the time to stop and read this post, if I'm going to take the time to watch your video or click on your website and go through the content, and then give you my name, phone, email, etc. What's in it for me?*

Many times, a lot of us business owners and entrepreneurs get so hung up on our offer, and all the features and benefits and all the things that we think are genuinely amazing about what we do.

Still, we need to consider the real problem it solves for our clients. Ryan always talks about it because he came from the mortgage industry, *don't sell them the mortgage; you sell them the home.*

In marketing, it's crucial to understand that people don't buy products or services; they buy solutions to their problems. Or in some cases, they pay for things that please them.

Therefore, it's essential to focus on the awareness of what your product or service does for your customers rather than the features and benefits of the product itself. This way, you can show potential customers what's in it for them and why your offer is worth their time and attention.

To effectively communicate the value of your offering, consider the big, hairy problem that your customers face and how your product or service can help them solve it. This approach is more relatable and will help you build a strong relationship with potential customers.

People don't wake up in the middle of the night and go,

> *"You know what? We should get a mortgage at 8.9% interest and pay on it for the next 30 years. That would be great, right, honey?"*

No, they don't do that.

They're like,

> *"Hey, we're pregnant. And if we don't get that extra bedroom, we'll be sleeping six deep in this little bed here, and that won't work out. What do we need to do to get that next home?"*

That's what we're solving for them. We're not selling them on the mortgage and the interest rate. We help them with the fact that they're going to have enough space to raise their family comfortably. That's what's in it for them.

That's that big hairy problem. That's the thing that keeps them up at night and that you can help them solve with your product or service.

Because again, when we listen to the radio, when we watch T.V., we are all okay with the occasional advertisement from a sponsor so long as we get some entertainment first. If the commercials bring us joy or educate us on the things that help us avoid pain, or get closer to pleasure, then we will sit through it.

Now, I know many of us are streaming on Netflix and some other places. But here's the deal, we look at ads and advertisements all day long. Every sixth post on scrolls in your timeline is an advertisement.

We're okay with being sold to, but only sometimes.

And that's where this following formula is going to change the game for you...

What to Post?

Being the Chief Content Creator of your business can take time, especially when deciding what to post online daily.

With so many options and the pressure to constantly develop fresh, exciting content, it's no wonder it can be a struggle. You want to make sure what you're putting out there resonates with your audience and adds value to their lives. But at the same time, you also don't want to run out of ideas or get stuck in a rut. It's a delicate balance, and it can be challenging to strike out everyday.

We never shy away from challenges. In this section, I will guide you on how to fix this problem forever!

When you're starting to put out the news, creating the content you're going to utilize to become the authority, to become that go-to person in your marketplace, you need to be very careful.

Because, as we've mentioned, you need to remember what's in it for the audience. And that audience wants to hear about the stuff you have going on, not just about your business. Our recommendation for coming up with content ideas is to use the E3 method.

{E3}

- Live your life and have awesome EXPERIENCES!
- EXTRACT the stories and lessons from those experiences.
- EDUCATE or ENTERTAIN your audience with them.

This is what you do in your daily life. That's what we're all here to do.

We want to have fun.
We want to go out.
We want to do the work.
We want to have badass experiences.
…and that's the case for most of us who choose to show up day in and day out as an example to the people in our lives.

Every day you have some experience. You're going through some interaction or transaction in which you could look objectively and extract some lesson.

The morning I had the idea for this book, we drove to the office in the cold. Very unusual for Texas, but we had work to do. We started having our morning meeting. In the middle of it, everybody's phones started going off and sending notifications about the impending weather that was headed to Dallas. Those of us who usually would come in and work at the office all had to have a serious conversation and say,

> *"Hey, it's not worth risking life, injury, etc., for us to try to be here at the office should the weather continue to get worse. Let's make the smart choice to cut the day short, spend the next few days at home, and be safe if the weather goes south."*

And that's okay because as a family of choice, a group that continues to work together, we trust and want to make sure that everyone's happy, healthy, and knows that it's not worth getting injured to be in the office for one day. That's a whole story and experience we had together as a business.

Suppose I share that with the online community. In that case, the audience who follow that story might find it:

A) relatable, because a lot of us have been in a situation where the weather has interrupted our day or our plans,
B) impressive, they may think this company cares about their employees. Because it says,

> *"Hey, if the weather's bad, don't show up. Don't risk yourself just to be here. We can all work from home. We're all adults. We know how to be responsible."*

Ultimately, this is what we're trying to do. We want to educate or entertain the people who are following us.

Sometimes those stories are fun, silly little things like,

> *"Oh man, there was an ice storm. We all went out into the parking lot. We slid around and saw who could fly down how many parking spaces on the ice. I'm glad none of us got hurt, as we couldn't waste time for long with all the work we had to do. However, it's always fun to take time as a team to be big kids."*

That's a silly story, or those stories could be more along the lines of the one that I just shared;

> *"Hey, let's educate our audience of business owners and entrepreneurs that it's okay to give your people time to stay home. It's okay to treat them with respect and understand that it's not worth them risking life or injury to be in the office when at this point in 2023, most of us can work remotely."*

When I mentioned that social media was a tool built by creeps for others to creep, this is how we leverage it to tap into the lizard brain of humans. We all have curiosity about the stories of others. That's why reality T.V. is such a draw for people. They love to live vicariously through their favorite stars' levels and character development.

Your timeline and content will be looked over by people worldwide, whether you like it or not. Be strategic about what you share, and be careful not to give away too much personal information or put yourself in a situation where you could potentially attract danger.

Social media, like all tools, is best used with caution and intention.

Never Gonna Give You Up, Never Gonna Let You Down...

*"GOTCHA B****!"*
– Dave Chappelle

know we have all been to the valleys of self-doubts, wallowing and thinking, why would anyone care to see what I am doing?

This is normal!

But recall the lesson we just learned; we are using our timeline to entertain and educate others. We are part of a larger community where we carry importance, and so are you! And believe me; people want to know what's up!

Your followers will find meaning and relatability in telling stories that educate and entertain your audience. They'll see you as someone they know, like, and trust. That's what we're trying to do with this whole process. As I mentioned, when we're watching T.V. and these movies, we don't mind taking a short break to hear from the advertisers.

Sometimes we enjoy commercials!

Think about the Super Bowl. People take time out of their life to show up and spend the whole day glued to the T.V. They don't even care about football. Still, they watch the commercials. Because of this, companies spend millions and millions and millions of dollars to put their commercials in that 30 to 45-second time slot. Banking on their creativity and ability to stay on their prospects mind with their message and offer.

That's how essential media marketing is, right?

It's one of the things that runs social media.

You're on these platforms because they want you to stay as long as possible and serve more advertisements.

After all, that's how they make their money on a free platform. If you're putting out content, it's okay too; every once in a while, talk about your product or service, why you're the expert, and why someone should feel confident doing business with you if that product or service is something that they need.

M3: The Media Marketing Method

If you turned on the TV and all you saw were advertisements, you'd change the channel. Treat your social media feed like a channel and use it as a way to keep your prospects and clients engaged with quality content, while throwing in the occasional reminder/ad for what you do and how you solve problems for the community!

If You Build It,
They Will Come!

"The privilege of a lifetime is to become who you truly are."
- Carl Jung

T hat's another thing that I think so many people are perhaps afraid of or don't have confidence in themselves. They're so scared to go and put their offer out onto the world because maybe they're afraid to be judged, or they're concerned that someone will make fun of them for it, or whatever.

I'm just here to tell you that if you have something that can help people, it is your duty to get out there and to provide it to the world, not to be spammy or to shove it down people's throats who don't want it or don't need it but to get out there and educate the world about your services.

Hey, this is what we do, why we do it, and here's how it could benefit you if you have X, Y, or Z issues. That's it.

You have to do that thing. If you do it well and you become the authority and the person that people know, like, and trust, you can live a pretty good life from that.

I'm here to tell you, as a guy who used to make 30 or 40 grand a year selling insurance and now makes multiple six figures in numerous different businesses, it all comes back to me focusing on how I will serve my clients.

How will I show up and support the people around me and help them solve the problems they're facing? Because the more problems I solve, the more money I make. And the bigger the problems I solve for these individuals, the more they're willing to pay to get that done.

That's how it works. But it's not about just selling them. It's about serving them by educating, entertaining, sharing stories, talking about things they are going through, and putting content out there for them to know, like, and trust you. And then, on occasion, saying,

"Hey, here's how to get access to the thing that I do the best."

Some of you will say,

"Well, Drewbie, I still don't know what to talk about. Maybe you could give me some categories that would be beneficial."

Well, here you are...

Stay true to **F.O.R.M.**

F.O.R.M stands for Family, Occupation, Recreation, and Motivation.

It was taught to me early on, and I'm here to reshare it with you. This is a straightforward formula. Again, everything we try to do is about keeping it simple because keeping it simple is what sells.

Don't discredit this stuff because it seems too simple to work.

The beauty of this whole process is that it falls back on human nature!

F.O.R.M.

FAMILY, OCCUPATION,
RECREATION, MOTIVATION.

Family

Posting about family is integral to connecting with your audience as it allows you to share a more personal side of yourself.

Pictures of kids, pets, or even llamas can bring a smile to your followers' faces and create a bond between them and you. We know a dude with llamas; he always posts about them. People love those kinds of posts. It's also important to acknowledge the "family of choice" – those close friends and relatives in our lives who are just as important to us as biological family members.

Sharing stories from these relationships that show the ups and downs but ultimately demonstrate resilience can be powerful for you and your followers. It indicates that you understand what it means to have strong bonds with people who are not necessarily related by blood.

Being vulnerable and open about difficult experiences in life can help build trust between you and your followers, as they will relate to such incidents. This could include sharing stories about loss, struggles during the lockdown, feelings of loneliness, or even personal growth milestones reached in recent months.

These moments of vulnerability allow people to connect emotionally, which helps break down barriers between individuals who may otherwise not interact with each other. Furthermore, showing how one has grown through tough times serves as an inspiration to others going through similar issues.

Sharing content related to family isn't just about providing entertainment but creating a sense of community amongst all types of families - biological, chosen, or blended - on social media platforms.

By sharing stories from different perspectives, we can promote understanding within our various circles while also providing support for others who may be facing similar challenges in their own lives. Social media users feel empowered when they know they are part of something larger than themselves – a large family connected by shared experiences regardless of age, gender, or race.

In conclusion, posting about one's family is essential for connecting with an audience on social media platforms as it allows individuals from all walks of life to find common ground over shared experiences that transcend beyond traditional definitions of family - allowing them to form meaningful connections with each other while supporting each other through difficult times along the way!

Occupation

Now that you are posting about your experiences, a good part of those will also include your work life. This is when you post about your occupation and your business. You get to talk about your product or service this small percentage of the time. There is an excellent trick behind making it all lead to sales: Telling Stories.

Tell your work stories.
Talk about wins, client successes, and case studies.
Whatever.

Creating compelling content for social media about one's occupation can be an effective way to promote your services and build an audience.

The first step is to establish a core understanding of who you are as an individual, what you do professionally, and how you solve problems for your clients. This will set the foundation for the stories you tell and the messages your posts will convey.

The next step is to create a strategy that outlines the type of content you want to make, when it should be posted, and where it should be shared. Knowing your target audience helps determine the type of content they respond best to.

For example, if you are a software engineer, then sharing tutorials and stories related to coding can help establish yourself as a thought leader in this field amongst other developers.

Once you have established a plan for the content you want to share, it's time to create it. This could involve recording videos or writing blog posts about recent projects or experiences that were successful for clients, highlighting members of your team who have made meaningful contributions, or simply sharing the stories of those whose lives have been positively impacted by your work.

Keeping in mind that visuals are essential when creating content can help capture people's attention quickly, so making sure any high-quality images used on social media can be beneficial.

No matter what kind of content is created, it's important that all posts are engaging and inspiring enough for readers to click "like" or share with their networks. Doing this over time will help build relationships with potential customers who may not have known about your services until they saw it shared on social media – increasing referral business while also making brand awareness and recognition within targeted communities online.

Recreation

What do you do for fun? That is not a rhetorical question… I want you to sit down and really think about it.

Talk about the things you do for recreation!

Do you hang out?

Do you go to parties?

Do you surf?

Do you ride bicycles?

Do you like to watch boxing matches?

Whatever you're into, there is a community of like-minded people who are also into that thing. Who more than likely either needs your service or knows somebody who could potentially need your assistance that they'd be willing to send to you if they knew, liked, and trusted you.

Sharing common interests is essential for business because it can help to create a sense of community and loyalty within a particular market. Companies can develop relationships that foster trust, build brand recognition, and ultimately increase sales by engaging with customers and followers who share similar interests.

When consumers are part of a larger group that shares their interests, they are more likely to spend time reading content related to the business, which helps to strengthen the company's reputation in their eyes. Additionally, by interacting with customers who share similar interests as the business, companies can gain insights into their target market and use that information to inform their marketing strategies.

Businesses can build relationships between themselves and their customers by showing customers that they understand them and are willing to interact with them on topics beyond just the products or services they offer. This will result in greater customer engagement and an increase in referrals from satisfied customers who trust the brand enough to recommend it to others.

Furthermore, when companies show that they understand what matters to their customers, this creates feelings of respect and appreciation which further strengthens loyalty toward the company.

When you start sharing about the things you are interested in, you'll be surprised to learn about and meet all the people in your community who share that interest. You might even go on to lead community events around that interest!

Online, my gaming and social tag have been @DrewbieRides for as long as I can remember.

Why?

Because I grew up riding BMX bikes and eventually, as I got older and afraid of hurting myself at the skatepark acting like a kid, I got into riding road bikes long distances. I am passionate about it, and because you need to stick to the things people know you as, it doesn't make sense to update my name or handles constantly.

As we mentioned, it confuses people, like bouncing from Job to Job; you want people to be clear about who you are and your mission or message.

Using social media, we have created cycling meetups for ourselves, and I've participated in multiple events orchestrated by social media communities. Events with thousands of attendees from all over the state meeting up to ride their bikes along a designated route. Tens of thousands of dollars in sponsorships sold and millions of impressions across social media sharing the stories.

You can do the same thing for your interests and hobbies, doubling down on the number of experiences you have and the stories you can share with your followers.

Tagging others you are participating with is another excellent way to increase your exposure by letting others who are connected to those individuals know that you have like-minded friends and interests.

Having them share your stories and content is just one more version of social proof to your audience of followers and the people you are trying to attract with this content and these stories.

Motivation

My ideal client is everybody reading this: entrepreneurs, small business owners, sales professionals, and folks committed to becoming the most excellent version of themselves. Within that, I know part of the entrepreneurial journey is going through the struggle.

When you first start this self-development and personal achievement process, you will feel great!

Then after a few days or weeks, you might start wondering if it's even worth it. This will happen because the results you seek will take time. The positivity and motivation you had when starting will be worn down by failure.

Rejection and the negative attitudes of people around you who don't want you to win will cause stress.

Sharing your motivation is about pushing through hard times and sometimes feeling as though the whole world is against you, wondering,

"Am I going to make it to the next paycheck? Is that vendor going to come through with the things I need to get this job done? Is that client going to stroke the check finally so that I can get to work?"

There are hundreds of stressors on the journey of an entrepreneur. There are a ton of things going on in our lives. Personally, the first thing I do every morning when I wake up is put on motivational content.

I listen to Ryan Stewman.
I'm listening to Eric Thomas.
I'm listening to podcasts that inspire me to get up and push through those hard times.

That's why I started my Crushing the Day Podcast, because I know everybody, for the most part, in my ideal client avatar needs that morning motivation, needs that push to get out there and crush the day before it crushes them.

I post motivation every morning because it's the first thing on my mind and something I recognize is on the mind of my audience as well…

The other side of motivation I will share is the power of sharing your story of health and wellness. I used to weigh more than 300 lbs and was only sometimes representing what winning looks like in the realm of fitness. As I went down the path of personal development, I shared my journey and struggles with weight loss and body dysmorphia.

Sharing these stories allowed me to connect with a new community of people who shared similar stories of overcoming weight loss and the struggle of body image in their own lives. The folks who read these stories would share with me, and others how seeing our posts inspired them to take action on their journey.

You never know who's watching your content and making life-changing decisions based on what you choose to share with the world.

Memes

If you haven't figured it out, I am "The Meme Lord."

It's something where I'm so dedicated to the life that I've tattooed it across my knuckles. I put memes throughout this book to further help explain my point. I created the Closer Memes course too. In it, I teach entrepreneurs and small business owners like yourself how to effectively create and use memes to speak to their ideal clients.

We've helped more than a thousand people implement this strategy. I've made thousands of sales with memes, thousands of dollars in commissions, and all from the tactics I share in a $47 course.

Who doesn't love a good meme?

If you look at your timeline on any social media platform, you will see a meme in the first four to five posts you scroll across. It's almost guaranteed.

Memes are one of the highest engagement-producing pieces of content you can use on social media. Just how the meme to the right has now engaged you. Everyone loves them. It's always a race to be the first among your friends to share a funny new meme. They transcend most taboo issues in a way you cannot do on video or with the spoken word.

Things like politics, religion, stereotypes, and personal interests can be taken to the line with memes. The secret to using them is understanding where to draw the line.

Memes can also be used to reach a very WIDE range of audiences.

It's one of the reasons meme marketing is such a powerful tool. If you have a good understanding of your client base and the things they relate to, you can create unlimited new memes to grab attention.

Knowing the interests of your potential buyer and what kind of things they are interested in is a vital component of any good advertising strategy. These should be things you are already thinking about and spending time focusing on while building your other marketing campaigns.

One of the reasons I enjoy using Memes in my sales and marketing process is the level of emotional triggers you can activate using a meme. As they say, a picture is worth 1000 words, so when you share an image that connects with your ideal client on a deeper level, you create a connection with them that far exceeds most other standard marketing methods.

All marketing comes back to imagery and the emotional triggers those images activate.

Going back to the days of old when rocks with painted images on them led weary travelers to their next destination or represented a local vendor location up the road. These days those painted rocks have been replaced with pop-up advertisements and sponsored posts on social media.

The way those businesses get your attention? Eye-popping imagery.

Something that grabs your attention and elicits a strong emotion. Preferably, a feeling makes you have an insatiable desire to pair it with the offered product or service.

Over the last couple of years, memes have become popular among the many societal sub-cultures. So much so that many large companies have taken on memes as their primary form of building rapport with fans. Chipotle, Mountain Dew, Wendy's, and even more corporate locations like banks and financial services have jumped on the meme train.

So many powerful companies are starting to see the value in memes because of how quickly they can get attention and spread that attention among their potential clients. Having the ability to create quick rapport with your customers and put them at ease during the initial opening of a sales conversation, you are setting yourself up for a highly lucrative business model.

Companies that struggle to open up the sales dialogue without getting the client into a position to feel like they've made their own decision ultimately work to stay open.

Building the Know, Like, and Trust factor with clients can be long and expensive. Having new ways to engage your current audience while attracting new, fresh faces to your business will help you create a pipeline that is constantly filling itself up with new prospects as deals are closing. The secret to staying in business long-term is a steady stream of new clients who want to support you—building the know, like, trust factor that much sooner in the process will make you wealthy beyond your wildest dreams.

I've sold thousands of them, ladies and gentlemen. People love memes. They're relatable. They're funny. People enjoy them. They laugh. They cry. Sometimes, posting the wrong meme could go a little too far and offend people. Don't do that...But post your memes!

#LOOKATMYMEAT

Let me take you through an insider story, and please don't mind me!

When I started making a little bit of money, going to fancy restaurants, and getting invited out to cool places, I'd take a picture of my fancy meals. Often they were expensive pieces of steak. I would take a picture of it, tell a story expressing gratitude for the meal, then end with something like, #LookAtMyMeat , and I started this silly little running joke. And then my beautiful family got me a smoker for Father's Day in 2022, and I've been smoking Texas briskets like a damn hoss ever since.

Every time I smoke a brisket, I post a picture of it, saying,

"Hey, look at my meat," and the whole world tunes in.

While it's cooking, I take short videos and create stories of the process, sharing that with my audience. Using the "Look at my meat!" posts alone sets us up for the future, where I'm going to start a whole business around smoking meats and showing the world my meat, and then putting my meat in people's mouths. And that sounds silly and not HR-approved, but guess what?

People think it's funny. It's not over the line. It's not going to offend somebody; at least, I hope not. Maybe it will, but more than likely, it won't. But it starts to create an emotional connection. It establishes that level of candidness and comfort.

> *This is someone who is interesting. This guy is online talking about showing the world his meat and putting his meat in people's mouths, and everybody is along for the ride. Here's a channel that I'm going to follow.*

Again, I'm doing it right. In that case, people are clicking on my profile, seeing these posts, going through my profile, and clicking on my Phonesites page. They're seeing all this and saying,

> *"Hey, Drewbie, can you tell me a little bit more about this Apex thing? Can you tell me a little bit more about your Closer Memes program? Can you tell me about X, Y, Z, whatever, right?"*

That's the whole goal. Getting someone to reach out and say,

> *"Hey, excuse me. I'm very, very interested in what you have to offer. Can I please get some more information?"*

Inbound marketing is what we are striving to build with our social media machine. A stream of inbound leads who already know, like, and trust us. You can do that with cold traffic and pay-per-click marketing. Still, it's not as effective.

Paying for marketing too early is also not financially possible for most entrepreneurs and sales professionals, which is why I will break down the difference between Organic and Paid marketing in the next chapter.

Organic Traffic Vs. PPC

"Where Da Leads At?"
– Me

This is where I reveal the magic of organic traffic and why it is a game-changer. We all have tried to buy leads or pay our way through promotion, but do you find it sustainable?

I don't.

I have learned through experience that organic traffic is a treasure trove waiting for you to unlock. This is also one of the simplest ways of lead generation. This section will compare Organic Traffic with Pay-Per-Click (PPC) leads.

Furthermore, you will learn the following;

- How can you generate organic traffic sustainably
- More strategies to keep your social media active
- How often do you need to post, and where to keep things running

- Some Bonus Content Strategies that will revolutionize your content

Organic traffic comes in from anything you do to get your message out that costs little money. This might include social media profiles, word of mouth, referral requests, etc.

On the other hand, paid traffic is just what it sounds like, which is when you are using a paid service to promote your product or service. These typically include newspaper, radio, television, and, more recently, social media advertising on platforms like Google, Facebook, Instagram, YouTube, LinkedIn, and Pinterest.

A crucial part of running a successful business is tracking the sales and revenue generated back to the different sources you use to generate traffic and exposure. By monitoring your KPIs or Key Performance Indicators, like lead source, closing ratios, and ROI(return on investment), you can figure out which parts of your marketing machine are working effectively.

Understanding your numbers and increasing your marketing ROI will make or break your business.

You can do that in cold traffic. You can pay Facebook **$5 - $100 a day** to put your Phonesites page or website in front of people who have no idea who you are or why they should trust you, and you might get a 4% - 5% conversion rate.

Hell, maybe even 10% if you're great at what you do in the marketing game.

Or you can spend some more time just sharing the things you're doing daily, putting your story out there, and attracting people to have an authentic connection with you.

Here's a secret that most people don't understand, it is when you start with a good foundation of organic content and social media mastery. The moment you start running ads, they become supercharged because you already have a seasoned pixel and audience that the algorithm can use to go and retarget to find new individuals with similar interests.

The problem I see is that folks will come in, build a funnel, throw a pixel on it, and start running random mass cold traffic to it. What happens is that you're confusing the algorithm.

You need to give it proper parameters to work from, so it's working twice as hard, spending four times as much money trying to figure out whom it's supposed even to be showing this offer to in the audience. But when you come in with a warm foundation, saying,

"Hey, Facebook, I have 1,000 active fans that follow me and engage with my content almost daily or weekly. Can you go in, take a look at them, and then find another 100,000 people like them and show my content to them?"

Guess what's going to happen? You already know. You will have a better opportunity to get your message in front of the right individuals.

Please don't sleep on the idea that posting this content and putting it out there is not going to further you along. Because here's the truth. When you start this process, it's going to take a little time.

You're going to wait to start making posts and getting hundreds of likes and engagements right away.

You're going to have to warm it up. But here's a beautiful thing. It only stops when you stop. In Facebook marketing, when you're paying for the system and you're throwing money into the machine, when you're playing the game, as soon as you're out of lives and you're out of quarters, they don't show anything anymore. GAME OVER!

But when you're posting to your organic timeline, this stuff literally lives on forever. It's in a giant database that can forever be searched, and this content lives 24/7. It's evergreen.

Think about that.

You stop paying Facebook Business and they don't show anything to anyone ever again, or you just put the free stuff out there and it lives forever for free. It's weird how that works, right? But this is the thing that the algorithm and what I think a lot of you are sleeping on is how simple it can be to really get yourself out there and to get your message in front of the right people. In the next part, I will show you how you can build that organic traffic effectively.

COMMUNITY

*"You Are The Average Of The People You Spend
The Most Time With."*
– Jim Rohn

B y creating a community around your brand, you have the opportunity to control the content that is being shared and seen by your ideal clients.

By maintaining a relatable and entertaining presence, you can continue to build a relationship with your audience, and establish yourself as an authority in your industry

By consistently providing valuable content and information, you can increase the likelihood that your audience will turn to you when they are ready to make a purchase, as you have established trust and credibility with them.

This creates a "loop of opportunity" as you continually build relationships with new potential customers and maintain those relationships with existing ones.

That's the power of creating your own Facebook community, just like the ones you're probably in right now. Guess what? We're using multiple groups to serve the community of awesome people who support our mission and to provide a support network to be here where you can continue to be educated and be entertained. We're following the formula we're teaching you here, in this guide in real-time. The same thing is possible for you. You could create a community group and build a massive audience of raving fans.

Hey, maybe you're super interested in WWE Wrestling. Start a WWE wrestling community for your local area, like WWE fans of Dallas. Or, if you can work with clients from anywhere in the world, open that group up to be something like WWE Fans Worldwide. A group like that would probably grow quickly and be filled with the most loyal of fans.

There's a whole load of groups like this out there, and I'll bet some of those people in those groups own homes, and I'll bet some of those people might need a realtor, an insurance agent, a roofer, or a contractor.

The fact that we have something in common, something relatable, and we like WWE Wrestling is just enough for my business to be in the line of know, like, trust versus the guy up the street who put his banner on the side of the road, and because we have that connection you like me. We have that relatability, therefore you choose to do business with me, instead of them.

Because when you have your own group, guess what? You control what goes in there. And because you're not competing against the billions of other users on social media, if you're in the group, you're only going to see what's posted by the other members in the group.

YOU'RE AMPLIFYING YOUR VOICE.

You're getting a chance to be seen by more people, ideal clients, and the exact people you want inside that community. They're seeing the content that you're putting out there. You are basically creating an endless loop of opportunity. Because right now, you're helping the people who are in front of you wanting to buy right now. The rest may have a three to six-month buying timeline. I don't know what your product or service is, but I know for us, it could be anywhere from 5% of people signing up right now today, with the remaining 95% of people that might have a three-to-nine-month timeline before they're ready to move forward.

If I just keep them in my group and I keep entertaining and educating them, I keep posting this content for them to feel included and cared-for, they may end up buying the product.

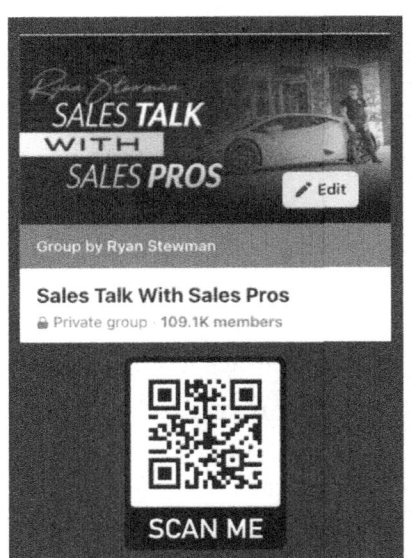

Here's a great example, **Sales Talk With Sales Pros**.

This group has over 100,000 members in it. In which we talk about sales, follow-up, marketing, job opportunities and growth. There are 100,000 people in that community who are our ideal clients. We pull millions of dollars a year in sales out of that group alone.

All because we focus on providing massive value and an engaging community for people to connect with and learn from each other.

Another practical example is **The Closer Memes** group, with just over 1,000 people in there. We talk about memes, and about marketing. Within that, I break down and share thousands of different meme templates and ideas with people so that they can go out and use memes in their marketing and sales process to make the kind of money you want to be making.

Ultimately, it's all about just providing value in there, while controlling the type of conversations being had. It's all about just putting this content out there and sharing it with the people who we know we can help. Because no matter how much we give you, at some point you're going to say,

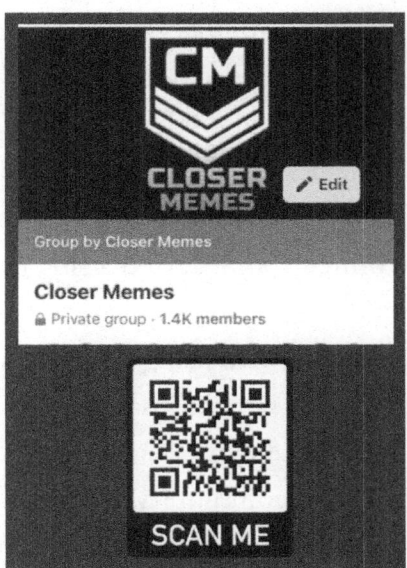

"Hey, I need a little bit more help. What does that look like?"

We have a product or service in place to help you get what you need to build that machine, to put these things in place and to understand how to tie it all together. Because when you start focusing on these things and you start getting more intentional, this is what happens.

I started my journey in sales back in 2013 with insurance. As I learned the product and became more of an authority in my local market my sales revenue went up.

In 2015 I got more focused on using social media to build our business and to generate more leads online by connecting with friends and family to create referrals.

In 2016 we opened a second location and my time was split between them teaching our staff how to get building so my personal numbers went down, but our team crushed it. You can see in 2017, I made $270,000 in sales.

But in 2018, it went down again because halfway through the year when I started learning marketing, I launched a marketing company and started a side hustle using Phonesites.

I started with using the things that I learned inside this very book that I'm here re-sharing with you guys four years later. Because what's made me successful is understanding that the more I pour into the community, the more I educate, and the more I entertain, the more value comes back my way in return.

The K.P.I's And Why You Should Be Paying Attention To Them...

Break Free Academy:

- 2013 - $105,501 / 199 Sales / $530 avg.
- 2014 - $173,428 / 342 Sales / $535 avg.
- 2015 - $272,955 / 440 Sales / $620 avg.
- 2016 - $221,692 / 310 Sales / $715 avg.
- 2017 - $270,167 / 365 Sales / $740 avg.
- 2018 - $215,942 / 319 Sales / $676 avg.

- 2019 - $925,482 / 746 Sales / $1240 avg.
- 2020 - $1,809,869 / 1414 Sales / $1279 avg.
- 2021 - $5,224,396 / 1124 Sales / $4101 avg.
- 2022 - $4,751,393 / 746 Sales / $6369 avg.
- Team 2022 - $1,813,251 / 379 Sales / $4784 avg.

Once I became an Apex member and started building my machine, I learned how to do these things in a more intentional fashion, almost a million in sales my first year, doubled it up in year two, tripled up in year three.

Last year, 2022, I did nearly $5 million in sales and had a team of guys underneath me that did about $1.8 Million, all because we got intentional, and we followed this very process every day on our platform, following these simple formulas. Then using that to drive traffic to our Phonesites pages, where we capture the information, and we put it into our sales and follow-up process. That's what you've got to do, right?

Maybe you're building the funnels, but not getting the traffic.

Maybe you're making the posts but not seeing the engagement you'd like.

Now you just have to get more dialed in and intentional, and you need to start measuring these things. Because if you're paying attention to the time and energy you spend using social media and building value, then you should get ready to intentionally convert it all into sales. You're going to start seeing the return.

So, who is going to take the time to add seven figures in revenue to their business because they're going to post once a day on social media?

All you have to do, just post once a day on social media.
Use these specific formulas.
Get very, very intentional about doing so.
I promise you, you will make more money, have more time, and enjoy more of your life than ever before.

In summary, to increase revenue and have more time, you should be intentional and measure your efforts on social media. Posting regularly and providing value to the community can help establish yourself as an authority in the industry and attract ideal clients.

Utilizing these formulas and being value-based can also lead to success.

Continuously learning and engaging with the community can also bring benefits.
Building a digital business card through software like Phonesites can also help in promoting oneself and connecting with potential clients.

Pick a Theme & Add It To Your Routine!

"You'll never change your life until you change something you do daily. The secret to your success is found in your daily routine."
- John C. Maxwell

H aving a set theme for your social media posts and committing to a routine will help you stay consistently at the top of people's minds.

A consistent message is essential because it establishes a sense of familiarity between you and your followers, encouraging them to check in with your page regularly. Posting content should have something related to the theme that ties it together, whether through words or visuals. It could be color schemes, topics, subject matter, or tone.

The next step is to create a consistent routine for when and how often posts are made. Doing this will help your followers know when they can expect new content from you while also helping with time management on your part.

You should create the schedule based on what works best for you, and make sure that there is enough time in between posts so that each post gets the attention that it deserves without being overshadowed by another one too soon after.

To ensure everything runs smoothly and efficiently, use a social media scheduling tool such as Hootsuite or Buffer. These tools allow you to create multiple post drafts at once and schedule them ahead of time in advance according to the frequency you've set up. This way, your posts are ready and waiting ahead of time while staying true to your theme. You can also use these tools to look back at previous posts' analytics to see what's working well for you and adjust accordingly if needed.

As a recap, having a set process makes it easier for any other team members (if applicable) who might be helping out with social media work because everyone knows exactly what needs to be done and when things need to be posted. As long as everyone follows the same protocol, there will be no duplicates or missing pieces that could disrupt the consistency and flow of posts being put out over time.

In conclusion, having a clear theme and creating a routine for posting on social media are essential steps in ensuring consistency across platforms so that people remain engaged with your content over time. Picking specific days/times when posts go out helps establish an expectation with followers who will visit your page more often looking for new updates; meanwhile, using scheduling tools takes the guesswork out of prepping multiple pieces of content quickly and efficiently, so there's no interruption in posting frequency due to last minute delays or lack of planning ahead of time.

Now I know a couple of the people who read this book will immediately come up with ten excuses as to why they don't have time to make these posts or start this process. You're right; go back to doing it your way and getting the same results you've been getting. See how that works out for you…

OR

You can commit to me right now.

A commitment that you will trust in this process. That's It!

Get your profile set up correctly, and dial in on the flow of your viewer's journey from the moment they land on your page to the moment they click on your funnel, raising their hand to say, "I am interested in learning more about you, and what you do."

The next thing I will ask you to do is make a post. For many of you, it will be the first post you've made on social media in a long time. That's OK!

Here's why…

It All Starts With One!

"Progress, Not Perfection!"

N ow that you have covered all the nitty-gritty of posting on your timeline, you must think about how often you should post online. Well, frequency and consistency are two important factors in social media postings. But, it is not supposed to tire you.

Allow me to share my own experience.

The next page holds my content posting strategy that has transformed my business. I currently use it for posting across all of my social media platforms.

Fair warning, it's going to overwhelm you.

You're going to look at it and immediately go, "NOPE!"

I get it; you already have about 69,420 things going on in your life, and adding many more tasks to your day is the last thing you want to do right now. I reached this level of content creation when I was years into the business and built a team to help me.

It didn't start that way, however!

In the beginning, it was just me, myself, and I. Responsible for creating my content and eventually being one of the first social media managers for Break Free Academy when I was an admin and creator for around 4-5 active business pages and as many private community pages.

So this is why I am here to remind you that it all starts with one...

JUST ONE POST PER DAY!

If you can commit to posting just once per day on the platform of your choice, you will be on your way to becoming a social media master.

As they say, in the entrepreneurial world, it takes 10,000 hours to become a master of anything. That same rule applies here as well.

If you make one post a day for the next 30 days, you will be well on your way to mastery!!!

Ninety days from now, as you've picked your theme, dialed in your routine, and built your machine, you'll start to recognize that you now have 100's of pieces of content you have created. You will feel that much closer to mastery.

Furthermore, if you've followed the process, you should have made quite a few sales, which is why you are here in the first place!

My Posting Routine		
1	Post 1-2 Times Per Day	Personal Facebook
2	Post 1-2 Times Per Day	FB Business Page
3	Post 1-2 Times Per Day	Private FB Group(s)
4	Post 1-2 Times Per Day	Instagram
5	Post 1-2 Times Per Day	LinkedIn
6	Add 5-10 Stories Per Day	IG/FB
7	Add One New Video Per Week	YouTube
8	Post 2-3 Blogs or Articles Per Week	Blog/Website
9	Record 5-10 New Podcasts Per Week	Podcast Platforms
10	Record 1 Tactical Training Per Week	Any Suitable Platform

It's important to remind you here that I am able to accomplish all of this because my routine and my time management are extremely dialed in. Not only that, but I've slowly built a team of people under me to help distribute and organize my content. You too can get there, but don't let it overwhelm you. Start with just one post per day, like I did!

Bonus Stuff

Because... "WE GO ABOVE AND BEYOND!"

I f you're reading this book, you're experiencing the process of content repurposing!

That's right...

The book you are reading started as a webinar I did for our Phonesites Users Group on Facebook. I took that webinar, transcribed it, had it edited by a professional, and then made a few tweaks to make the book you are reading now. It took me about 10-12 hours worth of actual work, and then the team I hired to help me finalize everything. The graphics, final review, and formatting for upload to the proper channels.

Less than 30 days from start to finish!

This book will generate leads for our business for years to come while providing massive value to our community for a lifetime. **This is called evergreen content.**

It's a compelling resource that I encourage you to consider implementing.

In the 21 Rules of Money, Ryan says, "Never work for the same dollar twice." It's a principle around only doing things once to get a return on the money you've already worked for.

This applies to your content online as well. Only a tiny percentage of people who follow you will see your content on any given day, typically about 10% of them.

So why wouldn't you want to save the stuff they missed and give them another chance to see it?

You wouldn't put on the performance of a lifetime and not record it for your friends and family, would you?

You may have and realize now what a considerable regret it is. Having those memories, being able to relive that moment. To experience the emotions again and again. It is a remarkable asset. Continue and extend this approach beyond your physical world and into social media. The returns and value will be massive. I've encouraged you to make just one post per day.

Start by saving your posts in a central location. It could be a google docs file, an Evernote drive, or any place you are comfortable with. Just make sure you are saving that incredibly valuable content.

From there, you can take that one post and record an entire video or training about the content and story.

How to Repurpose Content

One of the most prominent struggles entrepreneurs and business owners face is content creation. There are so many various platforms and ways to make content. The thought of it can easily be overwhelming unless you have a simple trick to help you turn one piece of content into multiple!

This strategy will help you spread your message across each of the available platforms and do so in a way that will resonate with the audience you are looking to attract and in a way that doesn't come across as spammy or repetitive.

Figuring out your audience and offer is the first step to content creation. You have to know what you will do to create messaging that will resonate best with your ideal clients.

Each of these questions will help you determine what content messaging to use.

What platforms are they on?

What kind of content are they engaging with the most?

When do they choose to engage with this content?

Once your messaging is locked in, the next step is to film a video. I know most of you are terrified to get in front of a camera. You're going to need to get over that ASAP. Video is one of the top ways to generate engagement with your prospects and is the starting point for creating multiple content pieces with one item. It's essential to practice your on-camera skills, especially now that many face-to-face meetings in business are held over zoom, skype, and other video conferencing platforms.

The book you're reading right now started as a video. It was a training I ran for our Phonesites Users group on how to use Social Media. The same content you've been reading this entire book!

So you've created your video... Now what? The following instructions will show you how to create several pieces of content from just one video.

#1 - Have the video transcribed.

You can upload your video to an online transcriptionist like rev. com and have the video transcribed to almost near perfection. You can then use that text for social media captions or blog posts for your website. OR, you can go crazy and do what I did… Turning that transcription into an entire book!

Creating blogs and similar content for your website from the transcriptions will increase your SEO rankings, which is extremely valuable for long-term growth. If you use them to write a book, not only will it make the whole process about 100x easier, you might be able to tell a similar story to mine about how you took a presentation or training and turned it into a Best-Selling book!

#2 - Make the audio recordings into a podcast.

Suppose you're doing educational or entertaining content, which it should be. In that case, you can take the audio and use it as a podcast. This is excellent content for folks who enjoy learning by listening but prefer to do so without the video. They may only have time during their commute or at the gym to take in the content. Using your audio as a podcast is a simple way to make this easy for your clients.

#3 - Ask your video editor to break up powerful quotes and mini messages into 30-60 second clips for your stories.

Taking short snippets from your longer video that accentuate the sharp, powerful points is a great way to create content to share with your stories. Stories only last 24 hours, so that you can repurpose this content multiple times over a year. You can also use the shortened videos for PPC ads.

There you have it!

You've successfully taken one piece of content and broken it down into five or more components that can be utilized on various platforms. Now that you have these different pieces of content, it's important to remember that you do **not** post them everywhere simultaneously.

Drip them out over a few days to not overwhelm those who follow you on multiple platforms. Start with the main video today and some stories on day two.

Drop the blog post a few days later and then the podcast a week later after that. You can see how this creates a perpetual cycle of fresh content to be seen by your audience without feeling like they see re-runs over and over of the same stuff.

The idea is to keep your great content fresh in your audience's mind without feeling spammy or overwhelming.

Now you've learned how to take one post per day, turn it into a video, and then use it to create multiple pieces of content that you can repurpose repeatedly!

Take the skills you've learned within these pages and apply them to your daily life. Implement the strategies and be consistent with them for the rest of your life. Whether you are using them to build a business or make an impact, these platforms can help you do amazing things for yourself, your family, and the community you are surrounded by.

Afterward

One of the most complex parts about creating content is those moments when you pour your heart and soul into something and get a minimal reaction.

Then you post a picture of a lady yelling at a cat and get 100+ engagements.

Social media is funny like that!

I'm here to remind you to keep going…

Keep putting out that content, even when you think nobody sees it.

THEY DO!

A lot of people like to creep…

They watch what you do.

They read every post.

They judge everything.

They never engage on a daggum thing!!!

So that post you poured everything you had into, that got 5 likes, it hit home with someone.

Your consistency is what inspires them to be better and take the actions they need to change their life.

So even if you're not getting the kind of response you had hoped for, remember that what you're doing makes a difference.

Not everyone is willing to do what you do.

In the long run, the message and seeds you plant now, will become the abundance you deserve!

People Who Follow Religiously But Never Comment Or Engage…

"I observe all that transpires here, but I do not, cannot, will not interfere. For I am...the Watcher."

Conclusion

I have poured my heart and soul into this guide. If you want to learn more, or have any questions, there are some amazing platforms where you can reach out. I told you, I'm using the stuff exactly as I got it laid out for you right here. Build your digital business card on Phonesites. All you gotta do is pull your phone out, and scan the little QR code below that's going to take you right to the page that I've built, MY digital business card. You can text me. You can contact me. You can follow all my other social media pages, buy my course, download my books, podcasts, and more.

To Learn More..

SCAN THIS QR CODE!

<u>**But more importantly, what I really, truly want to do for you today is offer you something special…**</u>

A PROFESSIONAL SOCIAL MEDIA BREAKDOWN WITH DREWBIE!

D o you wonder why some posts and accounts get hundreds of likes and comments and attract tons of engagement? While you spend time and frustration on posts that go into a black hole.

The reason isn't because they write better or have more interesting lives. It's because they use a proven strategy and repeatable framework.

This is the same framework I have used and taught to get hundreds of small business owners and entrepreneurs a more engaged audience and paying customers using social media as the foundation of their marketing strategy!

Here's the deal…

I'm offering a limited-time, 30-minute social media strategy session.

You'll receive a thorough analysis of your current strategies and personalized recommendations for optimization.

During this session, we will:

- Identify the significant weaknesses in your current strategy
- Review how to laser target your perfect customer
- Set milestones and tracking for progress
- Create a framework to follow and execute.

My goal is to provide you with actionable steps to start seeing the results quickly and tangibly. The results that attracted you to try social media in the first place.

Stop chasing down customers; instead, watch them come to you and ask to do business. To learn more about how they can send people your way.

This is not a new service, but something I usually reserve for a few high-ticket clients. The fee for this service is $1,500, but I want to try something different. To make a more significant impact for clients without those types of budgets. With my roots in small business, I get that.

So for the next 60 days, I'm offering this same service for $497.

I can't take on too many clients to prevent sacrificing quality and attention. So I'm making this available to the first 30 people who take action. Once the first 30 people act, I will close applications.

Sign up, and let's get you more likes, comments, leads, and sales without continued confusion or frustration.

As a bonus, you'll also receive replays from my top training and speaking engagements, giving you lifetime access to valuable content you can refer to and work from.

With my proven frameworks, you will see measurable increases in your results. If that sounds like a good match, sign up, and let's get started!

To Recap

30-Minute Social Media Review With Drewbie ($1,497 Value)

Crushing The Day Training w/Slides ($4,997 Value)

Sales & Follow Up Training w/Slides ($4,997 Value)

Closer Memes Course and Training w/Slides ($2,497 Value)

The Original Webinar Replay ($197 Value)

Original Social Media Mastery Live Event Replays ($497 Value)

Updating Your Algorithm Training ($497 Value)

Funnel Closer Live Replay ($297 Value)

That's $15,476 Worth Of Training And Guidance For Only $497!

…remember, I can only accept 30 clients at this time.

I really don't know if Ryan will ever let me run this offer at this price again.

Also… If you're not **100% SATISFIED** with our call, I'll refund your money and you can keep the bonuses for your time.

Visit: https://smmbookoffer.phonesites.com/
Or
Scan The QR Code To See If You Are Eligible

Join The Apex Family Of Choice!

Apex is a community of successful individuals who have transformed their lives by leveraging various platforms, including Phonesites. As a member of Apex, you can expect to grow your network, improve your financial situation, and strengthen your relationships, among other benefits.

Apex is constantly evolving to provide its members with the latest tactics and strategies for success. By joining Apex, you will be surrounded by a supportive community and have access to valuable insights and information that can help you become the best version of yourself.

Suppose you're interested in joining the Apex community and learning more about the benefits of leveraging platforms like Phonesites. In that case, you can reach out to Drewbie in various ways. Whether you scan the code, please send a text, or DM him directly. He is eager to help you become a part of this supportive community.

The purpose of Apex is to help you achieve the success you desire, regardless of what others may want for you. Apex has transformed my life in the past four years. I've become a better husband, father, business owner, and leader in the community.

By joining Apex, you will have the opportunity to gain clarity on your definition of success and build a machine that will help you achieve it. So, if you're ready to take the next step toward your vision of success, consider joining the Apex community.

You May Also Visit Our Website:
www.JoinTheApex.Com

Finally, I want to remind all of you that the success I have achieved and others in the Apex community have achieved is not just a pipe dream but a tangible possibility for anyone willing to put in the effort and trust the process. Don't let today defeat you; take charge and make it your own. The opportunity for success is waiting for you, so let's crush it.

CRUSH THE DAY BEFORE IT CRUSHES YOU ®

Acknowledgements

Once again, I want to thank my wife and son for their support and encouragement on this project. They've been with me by my side, watching this whole thing go down, and I am proud to show them what's possible!

Thank you to Ryan and the Apex family of choice! Your support on these social platforms is part of why I can launch a book like this and send it to the top of the charts. Your trust on this journey is paramount to ALL of our success. #WEAREAPEX

Thank you Mike Hardenbrook, the COO of Phonesites. You were instrumental in helping me put together pieces of this book, and without you letting me come into the group and help, this may not have come to light. I appreciate that you still let me come into work, even though I was technically let go from the staff years ago to pursue my position within BFA.

Best, Worst, Not an employee of all time?

Thank you to the editors and creative team who helped me put this together. I know it was a bit of a crazy project, and we moved extremely fast, but you all were fantastic, and I couldn't have done this without you. Apex Creative Team, thank you for the fantastic pictures and video footage. WE ARE APEX!

Thank you to the reader and, more importantly, the implementor!

If you took the time to read this book, please take action on everything you've learned here. It's why we do the things we do, to begin with. We want to show you what's possible when you commit to going all in and becoming the greatest version of yourself!

About the Author

Drewbie Wilson is a loving husband and father who pushes himself to live in excellence to set an example for those around him. At one point in his life, he weighed over 300 lbs before getting focused on his health and losing more than 100 pounds without fad diets or weight loss drugs.

An action taker with his finger on the pulse who focuses on service to others above all else, leading him to produce more than seven figures in revenues no matter what industry he has worked in. Not one to ignore a challenge, he looks to get out of his comfort zone as much as possible.

Drewbie has been in the sales industry since 2008, managing teams and helping businesses build and maintain client relationships.

From tech support in a software startup to Vice President of a multi-million dollar consulting company, he understands what it means to start at the bottom and work to the top.

Confidence and empathy are his superpowers.

By going all-in on every area of life, he strives to inspire success-driven winners to become the most elite version of themselves.

How does he do it?

Living by the motto...

"Crush The Day Before It Crushes You!" ®

LEGAL STUFF...
"My Attorney Made Me Do It"

Disclaimer:

No Earnings Projections, Promises or Representations

You recognize and agree that we have made no implications, warranties, promises, suggestions, projections, representations or guarantees whatsoever to you about future prospects or earnings, or that you will earn any money, with respect to your purchase of Crushing The Day products, and that we have not authorized any such projection, promise, or representation by others.

Any earnings or income statements, or any earnings or income examples, are only estimates of what we think you could earn. There is no assurance you will do as well as stated in any examples. If you rely upon any figures provided, you must accept the entire risk of not doing as well as the information provided. This applies whether the earnings or income examples are monetary in nature or pertain to advertising credits which may be earned (whether such credits are convertible to cash or not).

There is no assurance that any prior successes or past results as to earnings or income (whether monetary or advertising credits, whether convertible to cash or not) will apply, nor can any prior successes be used, as an indication of your future success or results from any of the information, content, or strategies. Any and all claims or representations as to income or earnings (whether monetary or advertising credits, whether convertible to cash or not) are not to be considered as "average earnings".

(i) The Economy. The economy, both where you do business, and on a national and even worldwide scale, creates additional uncertainty and economic risk. An economic recession or depression might negatively affect the results produced by Crushing The Day products.

(ii) Your Success Or Lack Of It. Your success in using the information or strategies provided at https://jointheapex.com depends on a variety of factors. We have no way of knowing how well you will do, as we do not know you, your background, your work ethic, your dedication, your motivation, your desire, or your business skills or practices. Therefore, we do not guarantee or imply that you will get rich, that you will do as well, or that you will have any earnings (whether monetary or advertising credits, whether convertible to cash or not), at all.

Internet businesses and earnings derived therefrom, involve unknown risks and are not suitable for everyone. You may not rely on any information presented in this book or otherwise provided by us, unless you do so with the knowledge and understanding that you can experience significant losses (including, but not limited to, the loss of any monies paid to purchase Crushing The Day products, and/or any monies spent setting up, operating, and/or marketing Crushing The Day products, and further, that you may have no earnings at all (whether monetary or advertising credits, whether convertible to cash or not).

(iii) Forward-Looking Statements. MATERIALS CONTAINED IN THIS BOOK OR IN MATERIALS PURCHASED AND/ OR DOWNLOADED FROM THIS BOOK MAY CONTAIN INFORMATION THAT INCLUDES OR IS BASED UPON FORWARD-LOOKING STATEMENTS WITHIN THE MEANING OF THE SECURITIES LITIGATION REFORM ACT OF 1995. FORWARD- LOOKING STATEMENTS GIVE OUR EXPECTATIONS OR FORECASTS OF FUTURE EVENTS. YOU CAN IDENTIFY THESE STATEMENTS BY

THE FACT THAT THEY DO NOT RELATE STRICTLY TO HISTORICAL OR CURRENT FACTS. THEY USE WORDS SUCH AS "ANTICIPATE," "ESTIMATE," "EXPECT," "PROJECT," "INTEND," "PLAN," "BELIEVE," AND OTHER WORDS AND TERMS OF SIMILAR MEANING IN CONNECTION WITH A DESCRIPTION OF POTENTIAL EARNINGS OR FINANCIAL PERFORMANCE.

ANY AND ALL FORWARD LOOKING STATEMENTS HERE, IN OTHER MATERIALS CONTAINED IN THIS BOOK OR IN MATERIALS PURCHASED AND/OR DOWNLOADED FROM THIS BOOK ARE INTENDED TO EXPRESS OUR OPINION OF EARNINGS POTENTIAL. MANY FACTORS WILL BE IMPORTANT IN DETERMINING YOUR ACTUAL RESULTS AND NO GUARANTEES ARE MADE THAT YOU WILL ACHIEVE RESULTS SIMILAR TO OURS OR ANYBODY ELSE, IN FACT NO GUARANTEES ARE MADE THAT YOU WILL ACHIEVE ANY RESULTS FROM OUR IDEAS AND TECHNIQUES IN OUR MATERIAL.

(iv) Due Diligence. You are advised to do your own due diligence when it comes to making business decisions and should use caution and seek the advice of qualified professionals. You should check with your accountant, lawyer, or professional advisor, before acting on this or any information. You may not consider any examples, documents, or other content in the book or otherwise provided by us to be the equivalent of professional advice. Nothing contained in this book or in materials available for sale or download on the website provides professional advice in any way. You should consult with your own accountant, lawyer, or professional advisor for any questions you may have.

We assume no responsibility for any losses or damages resulting from your use of any link, information, or opportunity contained within the book or within any information disclosed by the owner of this site in any form whatsoever.

(v) Purchase Price. Although we believe the price is fair for the value that you receive, you understand and agree that the purchase price for Crushing the Day products has been arbitrarily set by us. This price bears no relationship to objective standards.

DISCLAIMER PART 2: Social Media Platforms

The author of this book is in no way affiliated with the social media networks mentioned within its pages. The author does not control how these networks handle your content and usage of these platforms is subject to their specific terms of service and end user license agreement. By using these platforms, you agree to abide by their rules and regulations. The inclusion of these networks in this book does not imply endorsement by the author or any relationship between the author and these networks. The information contained in this book is provided for informational purposes only. The author is not responsible for any errors or omissions, or for the results obtained from the use of this information. The reader assumes full responsibility for any actions taken based on the information contained in this book.

DISCLAIMER PART 3: MEMES

This book uses memes as illustrations to make a point. The use of memes is protected under the laws of parody, which allows for limited use of copyrighted material for the purpose of commentary, criticism, or satire. The memes used in this book are intended to add humor and relatability to the subject matter, and should not be taken as endorsement or approval of any specific individual, entity, or ideology. The author and publisher take no responsibility for any misinterpretation or offense that may arise from the use of these memes and assert their right to use them in accordance with the law. The opinions and views expressed in this book are solely those of the author and do not necessarily reflect the views of the publisher or any other entity.

Made in the USA
Coppell, TX
18 February 2023

13055135R00083